Are *YOU* a

LEADER

Worth Following?

Ten Principles to Improve
Leadership Effectiveness

by
Wendy A. Kamerling

Goblin Fern Press
Madison, Wisconsin

Published by
Goblin Fern Press, Inc.
6401 Odana Road, Suite B
Madison, WI 53719
Toll-free: 888-670-BOOK (2665)
www.goblinfernpress.com

Design and typography by Sential Design
www.sentialdesign.com

ISBN: 978-1-59598-006-9
Library of Congress Number: 2006938230
Printed in the United States.

Dedications

This book would never have come into being without the encouragement and inspiration of several very important people in my life. It is to them that I dedicate this effort.

To my parents, Ed and Barbara Kamerling, whose love and support of me and my dreams have been a beacon and a touchstone throughout my life.

To Keith Wandell, who taught me what it means to be a leader.

To Mark Inkmann, who encourages me to discover my truth and live my own story.

To Margaret Harvey, whose loving support, suggestions, and enthusiasm prompted me to leave her dining room table and begin to write this book.

With love and gratitude,
Wendy

Table of Contents

Introduction

What are you passionate about? After spending twenty years in human resources at a Fortune 500 company, I discovered that I was passionate about leadership. In particular, I found that I was passionate about ensuring that people not only with the right skills, but people with the right heart, ascend into leadership positions.

Having the position, the power and the authority is really the easy part. Motivating people to carry out the mission of the organization with enthusiasm, creativity, satisfaction and speed, is the mark of the gifted leader. Sadly, those in positions of authority often lack the necessary traits and skills to energize a work group in this way.

The less gifted rely on intimidation, manipulation, and coercion to accomplish their aims. In my years in industry, I've seen the damage that is done not only to individual people but whole departments when they are supervised by a leader like this.

My goals in writing this book are lofty. I want to help improve workplaces. I want to make them places where people enjoy the work that they do, feel inspired by the challenges, feel that they are being treated equally and fairly, understand where they fit in "the big picture" and recognize that their hard work will afford them even greater opportunities. I want to participate in making workplaces more productive and more profitable because of the way each employee is treated. I want to help create leaders that are worth following.

My experience says that only with a commitment at the top of the organization can these aims be achieved. Do you have what it takes to make people want to follow you? Perhaps you supervise other leaders or you are in a position to hire and promote future leaders. Are you looking for the right traits and skills for your team?

What does your daily, on-the-job behavior say about what you believe and what you stand for?

- Do you encourage people to bring their ideas and concerns forward?
- Do you give clear, consistent and constructive performance feedback?
- Do you hire the best and fire those that cannot or will not perform to the stated objectives?
- Do you make tough decisions and then treat them with the compassion that they should be afforded?
- Are you honest in all you do and don't bend the rules because "you are you"?

Over breakfast recently a colleague who works with business leaders across the country said, "Remember that what you don't know, can kill you." As we will explore in the upcoming chapters, things like fear, lack of candor, lack of integrity, and lack of communication in organizations can prompt employees to hide problems, pass along defective projects, quit, or quit on the job. All these things cost your company money. All these things erode your effectiveness and your ability to deliver value to your shareholders.

As you read this book, think about your own leadership style and rate your leaders against the ten principles. What changes do you need to make to improve your workplace? Honestly assess your strengths and where you can improve your own behavior.

As I wrote this book, I looked at myself in the mirror. I clearly recognize that there are many areas in which I can improve my effectiveness as a leader. I am hopeful that by sharing some of my leadership mistakes, I can help you avoid similar pitfalls.

The vast majority of my experience is with large organizations. The examples and action steps reflect that bias. It is my belief, however, that the ten principles are universal. They apply to an organization of any size. They also apply to both formal and informal leaders.

Regardless of the size of your organization or the position you currently hold, I congratulate and encourage you on your continuing journey to become a leader worth following.

Your Story

You have a great product line, your customer list is the envy of all of your competitors, you have crafted a strategic direction that will reshape your industry and you have perfected the delivery of goods and services to your customers.

And yet, as you review your organization's metrics this quarter, you are incensed. This is the third consecutive quarter that earnings have been negatively impacted by surprises that surfaced during the quarterly forecast meeting.

In the first quarter, you had to take a huge equipment write off. When the project was launched 24 months earlier, the payback on the equipment was estimated at less than one year! Your Vice-President of Operations assured you that this equipment was going to revolutionize processing in your industry. It wasn't until the equipment was manufactured and shipped from the European supplier that the team realized that this equipment, due to differences in state laws, could not receive permits in four of the sites for which it was purchased. First quarter results took a beating and so did you...with the Board of Directors.

The second quarter looked like it was going to come in right on budget until it became clear that a programming error had inflated the invoices for two of the three months of the quarter. The Vice-President of Information Technology blamed the error on the change to the new electronic data interchange process that customers were demanding.

Not only were earnings artificially enhanced, customers who had overpaid invoices for two months were calling you directly demanding not only your involvement but interest on their money, as well. It took an extra three weeks to close the books that quarter and the Board meeting had to be delayed twice in order to assure accurate numbers.

This quarter, warranty returns of one of your standard products have tripled. Your new Director of Quality Assurance told you this morning that it is still premature to identify the root cause but early indications seem to point to a new supplier which was not adequately certified to meet the quality specifications. This product line has been a cash cow for you for four years. The firm depends on the revenue from this line to fund other, less lucrative parts of the line.

As you review other organizational metrics, you see that turnover in several key technical areas has risen to 12% per year. Three of the people that you have lost in recent months were leaders that you had your eye on for more responsibility in a year or two.

The last piece of bad news that surfaced this morning is a rumor of a potential union organizing campaign in one of your new facilities.

The Board meeting is in four days and you have no idea what is going on. The Board is losing its patience and it will be demanding better answers than you have been able to give the last two quarters. You drop your head in your hands and try to make sense of what has been happening in the last nine months. Have we grown too fast? Have we lost focus? **Do I have the right people in leadership positions?**

As you sit at your desk lost in thought over these most recent setbacks, your phone rings. Kevin, your now retired predecessor and long time mentor, is on the phone talking about some book on leadership. He really thinks you should read it. How do you possibly have time to read when you have all of these issues that need your immediate attention?

The Challenge

This book is written to you; CEOs, Human Resources executives, and all other professionals that are responsible for hiring and promoting organizational leaders. It has been written to challenge and expand your thinking on what makes a successful leader.

Certainly, any executive that works for you needs to understand his or her industry and function, be intellectually equipped, and have the energy and stamina for the pace of business in this global marketplace. These skills and capabilities are the price of admission in today's business environment.

To be successful, however, your leaders must have attributes that go well beyond these fundamental skills. They must exhibit behaviors that make people throughout the organization want to follow them.

The Motivation to Lead

Before looking at behaviors on the job, it is important to examine the core motivations of the people that you have assembled to lead your firm.

- Do these people aspire to corporate leadership because they see this career path as one that leads to wealth and a life of ease?

- Do they want to lead because they like to be "in charge" and value their own knowledge and contribution above that of others?

- Are they drawn to the status and influence that comes with positions such as these?

Your responsibility and privilege, as a leader of leaders, is to choose people who have the soul of leadership. Have you worked with a soulful leader? Do you recognize the key attributes?

- They believe that the mission that you and your team have committed yourselves to is worthy of their time and dedication.

- They respect and value the people throughout your organization that advance that mission every day.

- They deal with all of your stakeholders, both inside and outside the organization, with dignity and fairness.

- They understand that with great success comes great responsibility.

- They inspire others by their example.

- They create a legacy.

It is my hope that the following ten principles will help you select and assemble a team that not only meets objectives but inspires your entire organization to excel.

Part One
Setting the Standard

The Principles

Your bookshelves are lined with books about identifying and grooming leaders. I am a strong believer that while leaders tend to rise to the top of an organization, well-designed leadership development processes can speed their ability to competently assume greater levels of responsibility. Specific leadership training can also help these future leaders avoid the pitfalls and mistakes that may temporarily or permanently derail their careers.

In my opinion, however, there are some key leadership principles that you can't teach. Based on my experience, these principles are part of a person's character and, barring a major event or awakening, a person either has them—or doesn't.

If an internal or external candidate for a leadership position lacks one of these bedrock principles, offering them a position puts the credibility of your organization at risk.

These four principles are:

Live and Breathe Integrity

Respect and Care for People

Be Humble

Put the Team First

Let's examine each of these core principles in detail.

Principle One: Live and Breathe Integrity

I define integrity as doing what you say you will do. You are a leader that others can count on.

Corporate scandals like the Enron and WorldCom debacles have had debilitating ripple effects. They have destroyed the financial futures of employees and retirees. They have given rise to legislation that forces companies to spend money on detailed audits and extensive paper trails; further straining America's global competitiveness. They have destroyed trust in Corporate America and its leaders and made the public more wary of the stock market.

Perhaps most tragic is that they have eroded the faith that employees have in their own corporate leaders. Employees are left wondering about the wisdom of holding stock in their company, especially if their other retirement vehicles such as a pension or a 401(k) are dependent on their firm's financial success.

Recently, Harris Interactive conducted a survey for Age Wave, an independent think tank and Concours Group, a global consultancy firm advising senior executives. This survey, called the New Employer/Employee Equation Survey, queried over 7000 workers about various aspects of their workplaces. Just 36% of workers said they believe top managers act with honesty and integrity.

While corporate betrayals are devastating and far-reaching, the daily individual betrayals on the job are also very damaging.

Are your leaders inspiring confidence and loyalty by demonstrating their integrity on the job?

Admit Mistakes

Effective leaders admit when they have made a mistake or when they are wrong. They apologize when necessary. I have worked with executives who, when it became clear that they were wrong, simply began driving the work and the decisions in the opposite direction as they had been the previous day. No explanation, no apology.

For the employee, it is a bit like the emperor with no clothes. Should I ask what happened? Should I just adopt the new direction with no questions asked? The employee is left feeling confused and distrustful. Some employees stop working altogether thinking that the "wind may change direction again."

The leader has missed an opportunity to show her integrity by explaining why the decision was made and apologizing for any wasted effort that occurred.

Be clear that I am not suggesting "boss bashing." An effective leader does not explain the change in direction by saying, "Well, the idiots upstairs changed their minds again." Rather, the leader explains the change in a clear and objective way and emphasizes why it is important that the team realign its efforts.

Perhaps even more critical is when leaders make a mistake themselves. It generates tremendous empathy and loyalty when a leader is able to admit a mistake and ask the team for help getting the group back on track. Many leaders think that admitting a mistake is admitting weakness and that this must be avoided when leading a team. On the contrary, a leader shows tremendous strength when he is able to acknowledge that his actions were wrong and apologize to the group. This employee group will work diligently for this leader to assist him in producing the desired results.

Barry Nixon, President, National Institution for the Prevention of Workplace Violence, in his article *Creating a Respectful Work Environment May Be Your Best Defense*, states that supervisors who admit they are wrong can also provide a key link to preventing violence in the workplace.

Be True to Those Absent

The leader's credibility is also eroded when he says one thing to an employee's face and another thing when the employee is not around.

A classic example of this is in the performance management process. The leader will sit with the employee and tell the employee that he or she is doing fine and that there are no concerns. Or, as is often the case at the executive level, the boss will give his subordinate no performance feedback.

At some point it gets back to the employee that her boss has been saying to other colleagues that the project that she has been involved in is a complete disaster and he doesn't know what he is going to do about this employee.

An acquaintance of mine is grappling with a similar situation. His boss has indicated in the performance review process that everything is going fine. He is hearing through the grapevine, however, that the boss does not value his contribution. My colleague is left feeling insecure and confused and wondering about the wisdom of staying in his position. He has also lost trust in and respect for his leader.

Early in my career I began working for a new boss. I told him that I was taking a trip to one of our facilities to do some training as requested by the plant manager. He asked me about the training and its objectives. Upon my return, he asked me how it went and I spent some time with him discussing it.

I returned to my office and found a terse note from him in my inbox. He was upset that I had made the decision to go to the plant when a project that he had asked me to do was not finished. I stared at the note in stunned silence. How could I work for a person who stated one thing to my face and another in writing?

Similarly, be consistent in how you act and what you say when a peer is present and when he is not. A lack of consistency in your words and actions will invite your subordinates to wonder about your sincerity toward them.

Mixed messages like these create fear, anger, hostility and uncertainty. I have seen them lead to high turnover and lawsuits. I believe that other more serious consequences can also arise, including workplace violence and sabotage.

Don't Take the Credit

Effective leaders don't take credit for their employee's work.

One leader with whom I worked roundly criticized the work of one of his directors, saying that the time spent on the project was a complete waste. This criticism lasted until it became apparent that upper management thought the project was brilliant and it not only had application in one division but, in fact, should be rolled out across the entire firm.

Instead of an apology to the employee, the leader took credit for the idea with his bosses. Not only was trust eroded, considerable anger was generated toward this leader.

This leader also missed a wonderful opportunity to acknowledge the employee's contribution. Effective leaders look for opportunities to recognize exemplary performance both in one-on-one conversations with the employee and in larger groups.

Be Willing to Take the Fall

Allowing an employee to "take the fall" for an ill-advised or poorly executed project is another trust killer. In an extreme example of this behavior, I was asked to assist in the termination of an employee who had been working on a project that had never met expectations. As I discussed the termination with him, he told me that he had been surfacing his concerns about the project to his supervisor for months.

As I worked my way up the "chain of command," it became clear that the ultimate failure of this project had been predicted months before by a director three levels above this employee. Because this director lacked the courage and integrity to tell his boss that the project was doomed and the significant capital invested had been wasted, the employee at the "end of the line" took the fall.

Hold Yourself to the Same Standards

Employees watch their leaders. They know if a leader holds herself to the same set of standards that they are held to. Resentment can build easily if executives are allowed to be entertained by vendors while the rank and file must refuse all offers due to perceived conflict of interest, or if executives can travel first class while employees must book coach fares.

When visiting a company facility, effective leaders make sure they know and abide by the safety rules. If everyone in the plant has to wear safety glasses and ear plugs except the executives, the rules will lose effectiveness and the employees will resent the double standard.

Because the head of the operation may hesitate to correct a person in a higher level position, it is the responsibility of the leader to ask, "What personal protective equipment or specific safety guidelines must I be aware of?"

Maintain Personal Ethics

Effective leaders keep themselves above reproach. An excellent leader I worked with did not allow his son to accept a full-time position with his division's largest customer. Despite the fact that his son had worked there over a previous summer, had proven his value to the customer, and had been invited to join their company following his college graduation, his dad felt that other employees would feel that his son was getting special privileges.

Perhaps many of us have seen the damage done when the leader engages in an inappropriate relationship with a subordinate. Certainly numerous companies have been served with sexual harassment lawsuits when their leaders conduct themselves in inappropriate ways. Even if legal action is not taken, the company can suffer greatly from rumors, allegations of favoritism, employee turnover, and disrespect for the leader.

Disrespect for the leader can also surface when she is unexpectedly at the West Coast facility on a Friday just prior to the start of ski season or when the leader pops into the Florida facility in January.

Integrity is a bedrock leadership trait that people at all levels in the workplace have a right to expect. It is your responsibility as the leader to hire and promote people with this key trait.

Principle One: Action Steps

Action Step One:
Dealing with a Suspected Integrity Breach

Do you have some serious doubts about the integrity of one of your leaders? Have you discovered that something that he has told you is untrue? Have you uncovered a serious error in judgment? Before you take any other action, talk to this leader. Let him know what your concerns are. Be clear that if your suspicions are true, you are concerned about his future in the organization. Make sure that you listen carefully and sincerely to this leader's comments and explanations. He deserves a complete hearing on the subject.

Don't take action in the initial meeting. If the violation was flagrant and you do not want him on the premises, suspend him with pay while you complete your investigation and decide on your next steps. Disabling access to computer files, sensitive information or the company's premises are prudent steps to take during a suspension. Advise the employee that these precautions are being taken for his protection, as well as the company's.

Make your decision within two business days unless the investigation warrants more time. If you have suspended the leader, have him return to the workplace for the closing meeting with you unless you feel that his presence there is either dangerous or counterproductive.

If it turns out, based on your investigation, that your suspicions were not founded, let this leader know and apologize for any anxiety or concern the investigation caused.

Perhaps there was a violation but it was not flagrant enough for you to terminate the leader. Advise this leader that while his behavior was unacceptable, it did not rise to the level of termination. Document the incident, put a copy of the documentation in the leader's personnel file, and advise him that future occurrences of this type will lead to termination.

Should the decision be made to terminate the leader, work with your human resources or legal advisors to ensure that any lawsuit possibly filed against the company can likely be settled in the company's favor.

If, in the course of the closing meeting, the leader offers to resign, accept the resignation. Have it formally typed up while the leader is still there and have him sign it prior to leaving the premises.

Allow the leader the dignity of collecting any personal possessions that he might have at the location when other employees are not in the office. Ensure that there is adequate supervision to safeguard company assets.

Action Step Two:
Keep a pulse on your organization

One way to keep an on-going pulse of the organization is to implement the use of a 360-feedback tool. This tool can be developed in your firm or there are many that are commercially available. It can be customized to include questions on integrity, ethics, values, and on-the-job behavior.

A 360-tool solicits feedback from people with whom an employee works on a daily basis, including superiors, peers and subordinates. To solicit this feedback, companies send anonymous surveys to people who work with the employee. Most tools ask for both a numeric rating on a number of dimensions and offer an opportunity for raters to add their general comments. The consolidated feedback gives the employee's manager a much more comprehensive picture of this employee's daily behavior on the job. Many organizations use a 360-feedback tool as a part of the annual performance review process for all employees.

Make sure that the survey is anonymous and cannot be traced back to the sender or you will not get credible information. Ensure that you have a large survey sample so that individual results cannot be associated with the particular respondent.

By having regular 360-feedback available for your review, you can get a strong indication of the quality of your leadership team and its members' integrity.

Principle Two: Respect and Care for People

The most effective leader I have encountered in my career was a master at getting to know people. He was charismatic and energetic and he lit up a room when he walked in. I worked with him closely on a project and I remember so clearly how he took the time to not only learn the names of everybody from the janitor to the operations leader, he also knew about their families, their passions, and their jobs. He treated everyone as a teammate and a colleague, regardless of gender, race, or job title. It wasn't an act. It was genuine care for all people.

A colleague of mine was invited recently to join the two owners of her company for a dinner out of town. I laughingly said that four hours was a long way to drive for dinner. She answered with pride that she had been invited to drive with the owners to one of the company branches to honor two employees who had just completed their 25-year company anniversaries.

The owners in her firm respected these employees who had dedicated many years of service to the firm that their grandfather had started and which they now owned. They demonstrated their gratitude by honoring these long-term employees in a public forum.

Early in my career I was asked to assist in a plant shutdown. This plant had been purchased as part of a larger acquisition by our company just two weeks earlier. Upon announcement of the closure, the employees were understandably upset and feeling betrayed.

One of my assignments was to meet with each salaried person and explain the individual's severance package and last day of work. The first person I met with was a dedicated, long-service employee who had worked in that plant and its predecessor nine years longer than I had been alive. The meeting was heated and hostile and I struggled throughout to maintain my composure.

Upon the conclusion of that meeting, the PA system announced that a call was holding for me. I picked it up, still distressed and near tears. On the phone was my project leader, who not only had anticipated that the meeting would be stressful, he made sure that he called me. On the call, he took the time to remind me of our plan: why the plant needed to close, the strategy for the overall business, and how this plant closure ensured the economic health of the entire enterprise. Never mind that he was in a different facility in a different time zone. He called when he knew that one of his team members needed encouragement.

Certainly, many of the decisions made in Corporate America today are difficult. In order to remain competitive, companies have had to outsource jobs, cut benefits, reduce wages, and close plants. How a company executes these difficult decisions speaks volumes about the compassion and the effectiveness of its leaders.

These actions also predict the future loyalty of an organization's employees. If the "survivors" of a downsizing feel that the affected employees have been treated with fairness and respect, they are much more likely to remain engaged and active in the business.

An effective leader takes control of a downsizing situation. She talks to the employees after the action. She explains why the action was necessary, why it was done the way it was done, what provisions were made for the former employees and, most importantly, she paints the vision for the future. This leader helps employees move past the hurt and betrayals that they are certainly feeling by helping them understand why the decision was necessary.

I recently assisted a company that had to close a manufacturing facility in an effort to remain competitive. The work was moving to another country. I was impressed by the compassion the facility manager had for his employees. He ensured that on the day of the announcement, each of the employees in the facility received a written document that identified their last day of work and their severance pay. Because a large percentage of the workforce did not speak English, he made certain that the letters were produced in two languages.

In addition to written notification, the facility manager arranged to have several human resources people on hand to meet with each employee individually to discuss the closing, the timing and how the severance was derived. Interpreters were on hand to assist with the communications.

The facility manager also arranged to have human resources people and interpreters on hand the day after the announcement in the event that an employee needed to have something clarified the next day.

Throughout the two-month closure process, the facility manager gave his employees time off for interviews, brought in other employers to discuss positions that were available in the community, and had people on hand to assist employees in filing for unemployment benefits.

This leader diffused a potentially hostile situation by reinforcing to the employees that even though the plant was closing, he still considered them valuable members of his team. Throughout the closure process, he continually demonstrated his genuine respect and care for people.

Barry Nixon, in *Creating a Respectful Environment May Be Your Best Defense*, talks about the workplace being increasingly dysfunctional due to worker job insecurity and anxiety. He indicates that workers are becoming more volatile as a result.

Even our language in Corporate America today has begun to devalue the human being. By referring to employees as "human capital," we reduce people to the level of machinery or lines of credit. In his article on workplace violence, Nixon put it this way, "Management's view of people has changed from thinking of employees as assets to be developed, to thinking of people as costs to be reduced or commodities who possess certain skills to be bought or sold."

Nixon goes on to advocate that companies develop the "right corporate culture." He defines this culture as one in which leaders:

- Get to know employees and listen to them
- Give employees a forum to air their concerns
- Resolve concerns in ways that are considered fair
- Support and value their people

Nixon makes a compelling argument when he states that by treating people with respect, companies are less likely to experience episodes of violence in the workplace.

I recently attended an employment law update at the headquarters of a major national law firm. The senior labor attorney who was discussing employment terminations indicated that many lawsuits over employment terminations start with disrespect by a manager. Certainly, terminating an employee can be very difficult and very emotional. If, however, the manager has respectfully laid out the expectations that he has of the employee, has calmly identified where the employee is not meeting expectations, and candidly discussed what the consequences of continued lack of performance are, an employee will be much better prepared to handle the news of an employment termination and much less likely to file a lawsuit or resort to inappropriate or violent behavior.

In my experience, a leader cannot be trained to respect and value a person. Leaders cannot be taught to learn and use a person's name or look people in the eye or ask about their families. This is genuine respect and love for people—a critical leadership trait that springs from the soul.

Principle Two: Action Steps

Action Step One:
Add Values or Behaviors to the Performance Management Process

You may want to consider adding respect for fellow employees as part of your performance management process. Increasingly, companies are adding behavior or values based dimensions to their performance review process to reinforce that "how the job is done" is as important as "if the job was done."

As the leader of your organization, you can make a strong statement about valuing and respecting others by making it part of your formal review process.

Action Step Two:
Adopt and Communicate a "Zero Tolerance Policy"

You can make another strong statement about the value of each employee by issuing a "zero tolerance" message to your employees. A zero tolerance message might be in the form of a policy that describes how fellow employees are to be treated and the complaint mechanism available if an employee feels they have not been treated in accordance with the policy.

Action Step Three:
Assess the Human Resources Function

Consider the effectiveness of your human resources function. Do you have employees in the department who can effectively hear both sides of a disagreement, conduct a thorough and fair investigation, decide on an equitable, defensible and consistent solution and implement it with compassion and candor? Your human resources department can be a great ally or a tremendous liability as you seek to improve the level of respect in your organization.

A recent phenomenon in the effectiveness of the human resources function, according to Barry Nixon, is that there appears to be a correlation between the change from a human relations to human resources approach (the 'science' of managing and utilizing people as resources) and the rise in violent incidents."

Action Step Four:
Set Expectations and Model Behavior

Meeting with your leaders and setting your expectations about how you expect they will treat employees throughout the organization is another powerful message. Model the behavior that you want. If you are seen talking with employees and their spouses at company events or asking an operator how their machine is running on a given day, your leaders will recognize this as a key value in your organization.

Action Step Five:
Handle Difficult Situations with Planning and Compassion

If your company is faced with a downsizing situation, consider how your team can show respect and compassion to those who are affected. Things to consider include:

- Ensure that all of your leaders have consistent communications about what is happening, why it is happening and when it is happening. Trust will be eroded if employees hear different messages from different people.

- Be prepared to give affected employees information about their last day, their separation pay, and how their benefits will be affected. While employees will be unable to absorb this information on the day they are notified, well written communications that they are able to take home will answer their questions as they arise. Make sure that verbal and written communications are available in multiple languages, if necessary.

- Consider having experts on hand to discuss benefits, outplacement options, resources available in the community, unemployment benefits, etc.

- Do not announce layoffs or closures at 4:00pm on a Friday afternoon. Monday or Tuesday is preferable as it gives those affected the opportunity to access banks, benefits specialists, and other professionals in the days immediately following the action.

- Give notice whenever possible

- Immediately following the downsizing meet with any remaining employees. Discuss the reasons for the decision and what provisions have been made for the exiting employees. Answer employee questions as honestly as you can. If you cannot commit to the downsizings being over, don't say that they are.

Action Step Six:
Recognize Employees

Another way to demonstrate that employees are valuable in your organization is to provide various recognition vehicles to highlight exemplary employee performance. There are many kinds of recognition processes in place, ranging from very simple to very complex. The type of process that you select will depend on what type of behavior you want to reinforce and what is important to your company.

For organizations that want to promote teamwork between departments, you may develop a recognition process that allows an "internal customer" to nominate a fellow employee. If your organization wants to drive innovation, you may want to honor employees who receive patents or patent disclosures.

Many manufacturing firms recognize exemplary safety performance with employee lunches served by company executives.

There are numerous options from which to choose. As the leader, you can work with your team to decide what organizational value or behavior you want to reward and then set up a system to recognize it.

Principle Three: Be Humble

Arrogance has become epidemic in our corporate institutions. A division president in a major supplier to the telecommunications industry remarked to me recently that leaders "would do well not to take themselves so seriously."

Arrogance—the supposition that you either know everything already or that you are above certain things—can hurt a company in a myriad of ways.

The increasing competitiveness of the retail industry has changed the way that suppliers and their customers interact. Long-time suppliers have found that after decades of doing business with a major customer, the entire line of business is being put out for bid.

In a company I worked for, a major retail customer decided to rethink its entire sourcing process. The customer hired a consulting firm to help decide which products would be put out for bid to see if a better value package could be acquired from the broader market. The product our firm supplied was selected for the bid process.

The leaders of the firm I worked for were incredulous. They had done business with this retailer for decades. Together they had reshaped how the industry went to market, how sales were tracked, and how orders were replenished. Together they had built the strongest brand in the industry. Given this long history, the leaders of my firm could not believe that this was a serious threat. Even as they participated in the bid process, they did not realize the severity of the situation.

The firm lost 100% of the business with this long-time customer, which represented 23% of its annual revenue. The business was awarded to its fiercest competitor. In the weeks and months that followed, thousands of employees lost their jobs as departments and plants were shuttered. This company, like many others, learned the hard way that the arrogance of resting on a past relationship and failing to honor the new thoughts and directions of customers can cost business.

In this circumstance, the situation ended happily. The leaders of the firm recognized that they had wrongly and arrogantly assumed that the business would always be theirs and that a lower price from a competitor would not tempt this major customer. I was impressed that the members of the leadership team admitted to themselves and to the customer that they had misread the situation and committed themselves to regaining the customer's business.

Over the course of the next several years, the company changed its sales and marketing approach with not only that customer, but with all its customers. It made certain that each customer felt like an important partner. Those in leadership roles who could not make that shift to an attitude of humility were removed from key positions.

The firm not only regained all of the large customer's business, it began increasing its overall market share. Today it is the undisputed world leader in its industry.

Key humility skills are critical, not only with customers but with employees as well.

Listen

Perhaps the best method for demonstrating a humble attitude is by listening attentively. As the leader, you are saying, "While I may not agree with what you are saying, our relationship is important enough to me to hear you out."

I have worked with many unionized facilities over the years and I was always frustrated when I heard that instead of discussing a situation with an employee and perhaps reviewing the collective bargaining agreement for guidance, a supervisor would say, "You don't like it, file a grievance." That arrogant attitude costs companies time and money.

I worked with a very talented young professional who had been recruited from a large consulting firm. Soon after he joined the company in a leadership role, it became clear that he disagreed with a number of the decisions that had been made prior to his arrival. Despite numerous conversations with his boss about the strategy and the direction the company had charted, he felt so strongly that he was right and other key leaders were wrong that he made it a habit of going around his boss to the leader of the division. This arrogance caused him to lose the support of not only his boss, but that of many of his peers as well.

Ask

Being humble means being open to the fact that someone else might have a better idea than you do. Asking for their opinions shows employees that the leader recognizes that the people who do the work usually have the best and most relevant ideas.

Don't ask via a suggestion box or a survey or a write-in campaign. Ask people. Talk with them. Is scrap too high? Ask for suggestions. Is work-in-process time twice the industry average? Ask for ideas. Are error rates on your invoices increasing? Ask the people doing the work for help.

If the leader asks sincerely, gives people feedback on their suggestions, gives them credit for their ideas and thanks them, she will be amazed at the quality of their thinking and the depth of their commitment.

If, on the other hand, she asks because she read somewhere that it was a good thing to do and she never implements an idea or lets people know what became of their suggestions, she has guaranteed that they won't respond the next time.

Acknowledge

I find it incredible that some leaders cannot even seem to be bothered with saying hello to a subordinate in the hallway or getting to know someone new. Nothing screams arrogance louder than employees feeling that the leader "is too good" to speak to them.

When I have coached leaders on this, they often say that they are just shy or they have something else on their mind. Leaders must recognize that perception matters. Be approachable—it is your responsibility.

Being a "humble leader" or a "servant leader" seems to be in vogue now. It is not, however, a teachable trait. Neither is it a cloak your leaders can put on when they walk in the door. Your leaders either have a spirit of humility or they don't. They either think it is a privilege and an awesome responsibility to lead people and ask them to trust their direction or they don't.

Leaders who don't are not worthy of the role.

Principle Three:
Action Steps

Action Step One:
Adopt an "Open Door" Policy

Establishing an "open door" policy throughout your leadership team lets your employees know that what they have to say is important to you and to your company. When a genuine open door policy is implemented, employees feel free to talk to members of the leadership team without fear of reprisal for "not going through the chain of command."

Ensure that if a concern or an idea is brought to a member of the leadership team, it is given the appropriate follow-up. In general, employees don't mind when the answer is no, as long as the answer is explained in a clear, credible, and timely way.

Many supervisors who are out among their employees a great deal find it helpful to carry a small notebook and a pencil. That way, if an employee stops them with a question or a suggestion, they are able to jot a note and not rely on their memory.

As the leader, take time to meet with your leaders on a regular basis to "air out" the concerns that each of you is hearing. In addition to making everybody feel that they are involved in what is going on, you will quickly see which of your leaders your employees are avoiding.

Action Step Two:
Host Regular Communication Meetings

Regular communication meetings that allow employees to ask you questions about the business give you the opportunity to understand what your employees are concerned about. They also demonstrate to your employees that you are approachable and willing to take the time to engage in a discussion with them.

You may be thinking, "I don't have time for all of this employee nonsense. I have a job to do!" Yes, being open to employees and to their suggestions does take time. It is my belief that spending the time up front will save you the time of hiring replacements for your disgruntled employees, defending against a union campaign, or serving as a witness in a lawsuit.

Action Step Three:
Model Humility

Again, you as the organizational leader can model humility in your workplace. For example, solicit your leadership team to join you in a celebration of the organization's successes by serving a meal to your employees. If you or a member of your leadership team is "too good" to flip a burger or pour some soft drinks, your firm has the wrong leaders.

Look around your workplace. Are there perks that are only available to the leadership team? Do you have executive parking or an executive lunchroom? Eliminating things that divide employees into "have and have not" categories will help drive an atmosphere of humility in your organization.

Does your organization host summer picnics or holiday parties? Watch the behavior of your leaders at these events. Do they talk together, eat together, and basically ignore the rest of the guests? A humble leader will get out and mingle with people. Yes, this may push you outside of your comfort zone.

You might forget a spouse's name or call an employee by the wrong name. That's OK. The point is that you are out among your workforce. You are saying that "even though I may have a bigger job than you do, I recognize that without you, we can't be successful."

Principle Four: Put the Team First

Perhaps we have all worked with individuals who work hard to advance themselves rather than advance the objectives of the group. Such people are concerned with how they look and how they are perceived and have little or no concern for the work group.

Typically these employees are insecure. They feel that in order to be considered competent and looked at for promotion, they have to be in the limelight. They need to ensure that the right people see them. As a result, they are poor team players. Others on their project teams resent these "glory hogs," who take credit for the group's work, blame others for mistakes, or abandon a group decision if they see that the political winds are blowing in the opposite way.

I was once negotiating a contract in a unionized facility and we were spending a great deal of time talking about an unpaid provision that the union wanted to put in the contract. The company did not want to make a stipulation that jobs would be held open if an employee was employed elsewhere. In time, it became clear that we were arguing about a provision that affected only one person in the whole plant—the union president.

Although they maintained "solidarity," I often wondered how the rest of the union members on the bargaining committee viewed their leader, who was so obviously concerned with his own issue ahead of theirs.

A leader worth following puts her wants and needs second to those of the group. I have seen this type of leadership demonstrated in several instances.

An engineering executive in one firm in which I worked was asked to give up his best performer. The employee was deemed a key talent in the organization and as a result, he needed to work on a broad range of assignments. While losing this key employee was going to cause considerable hardship in his own department, this leader recognized that over the long term, the entire company would be stronger due to his sacrifice.

In another instance, a leader in the manufacturing function of a Fortune 500 company was asked to dramatically expand the number of products his facilities were producing. He recognized that all of these new products would add significantly to the complexity of his operations and erode the efficiency, cost, and productivity metrics by which he was measured. This leader worked with the sales and marketing team to understand the long-term customer benefits the company would derive and he supported the changes even though they made his job more difficult.

Unfortunately, I have also experienced a lack of teamwork on the job. In a project I was leading many years ago, I was working with engineering, manufacturing, and an outside vendor to produce up-to-date training materials for the operators in our plants. Upon receipt of the final draft from the vendors, I asked a teammate in engineering to have the information reviewed for accuracy. Following a lengthy engineering review, the outside vendor put the information in final form and distributed it throughout the multi-plant network.

Almost immediately, I began to get calls from the engineering department stating that some of the information was wrong. I went back to my teammate to ask what the problem was and he admitted to me that he didn't think that the project would ever be finished, launched or accepted by the plants so he did not put his best and most knowledgeable people on the review. This lack of teamwork caused a significant amount of confusion in the plants and forced an expensive rewrite of material.

For the most part in my career, however, I had the great pleasure of working on leadership teams in which each member took this teamwork principle very seriously. We were a team and we made team decisions. We often said to each other; "If I have to go to war—you are the people I want to go to war with."

Being a team player is another trait that, in my opinion, cannot be taught. It is an attitude that is inherent in a leader's style. It permeates decision-making and on-the-job behavior. It demonstrates the grace of cooperation and collaboration.

Principle Four:
Action Steps

Action Step One:
Create Opportunities for Collaboration

As the leader of the organization, it is your job to build an effective team. Meet regularly with your leadership team to share significant developments in the operation, as well as to hear from your team on what is happening in their respective departments.

If you are concerned about specific leaders being unable or unwilling to work together, assign them to a common project. Make them jointly accountable for the results. Ask for periodic status reports to assess progress and teamwork. In the final report, ask the leaders to describe the compromises that each of them had to make in order to achieve the objective. Did these leaders sacrifice some success, notoriety, or accolades for their function so a better overall result could be achieved? What sort of language did they use when presenting their results? Was the presentation peppered with "I" statements or did the leaders acknowledge each other and team members who may have helped them?

Listening to your leaders describe their participation in a group project is an excellent way to determine whether or not you have team players in your leadership group. An excellent leader with whom I worked closely would interrupt a subordinate's presentation if the leader was using "I" or "them" too often. He would ask, "Don't you mean 'We'?"

Observing your leaders in a group dynamic is also a good way to determine whether or not you have team players. As you build your organization's strategic plan or work together to identify the values and behaviors you want your employees to exhibit on the job, watch the interaction between the members of your leadership team. Do you have leaders who dominate and don't listen to anybody else's ideas? Do you have leaders who withdraw and don't participate at all, feeling that the session is a waste of their time?

Action Step Two:
Model Teamwork

How are you demonstrating your commitment to teamwork? In one company I worked for, the general manager of the group mandated that his team attend a safety leadership workshop. He had determined that his team did not have the focus that was required to lead a successful safety effort. I remember clearly that he walked into the workshop at the beginning and set his expectations for our participation. Then he left and was gone for the entire day. He came back in at the end of the day to wrap up the session and let his leaders know that he did not feel that we were committed to safety and that he had high expectations for improved safety performance. Several of us who attended the session talked later and we agreed that despite the fact that the seminar contained a great deal of helpful information on how to lead the safety effort in our company, the main message we received was that our boss was not in this with us. He was holding us to a standard to which he was not willing to hold himself.

Action Step Three:
Host a Teambuilding Session

If you feel that you have leaders who are committed to teamwork but at times are working at cross purposes, consider hosting a teambuilding session. Teambuilding can follow many formats. Some firms have found success with challenging outdoors activities. As a leader you need to recognize that some of these activities might serve to divide your team rather than unify it. If you have people on your team who are older, non-athletic, or physically challenged in some way, a rigorous physical event is not the right choice.

When I started working for a new boss early in my career, I lived in fear that, like his last leadership team, he might take our team on an Outward Bound teambuilding exercise. As the only woman in the group, I envisioned myself with a group of ten male teammates carrying a 50-pound pack, pitching a tent in the dark, and digging my own latrine, with not a hairdryer in sight. Perhaps this would appeal to some. It did not appeal to me.

On the opposite end of the spectrum, some leaders host sessions during which colleagues talk about what is going right and what needs to be improved in the way that they communicate with one another. While these types of sessions can be effective with certain types of groups, I found that when working in a manufacturing setting with mostly "Type A" leaders, these sessions were awkward and unproductive.

By working with a qualified industrial psychologist or human resources professional, you can select the best format for the type of leadership team that you have. An outside professional could also facilitate the session for you, leaving you free to participate as a full member of the team.

In my experience, the best teambuilding sessions are developed around trying to solve a common business problem or capitalizing on an emerging opportunity. One of many outcomes of the session will be better teamwork.

Part Two
Building the Culture

The Principles

All leaders work within an existing organizational culture. The most effective leader recognizes the nuances of the culture, how to manage within it, and how to change it to produce the results that he wants.

In this section, I will highlight four culture principles:

Eliminate Fear

Manage Consensus

Be Candid

Communicate

Principle Five: Eliminate Fear

Is there a culture of fear in your workplace? Do employees try to "keep their heads down" rather than try to come up with creative new ways to sell products or satisfy customers? Nothing will erode the effectiveness of a leader faster than fear. Fear stifles creativity, blocks risk-taking, promotes finger-pointing and kills cooperation.

Realistically, most companies have some fear in their workplaces. The volatile nature of today's workplaces creates anxiety as jobs are consolidated and outsourced.

A more dangerous kind of fear, I believe, is the fear of the leader.

Bosses who inspire fear in their subordinates are so driven by their sense of the "right way" to do things that they shut off healthy debate. It takes incredibly strong subordinates to endure a lengthy and heated lecture from their leader and then to respectfully disagree because the leader lacked a critical piece of information. In a fear-based culture an employee in that situation will shrug and think, "OK, if that's the way he wants it" rather than challenge the erroneous assumption.

Some leaders seem to have the sense that if they aggressively question, berate or degrade an employee in front of his or her peers that somehow they have set an example for the others in the room. Perhaps they feel the message that they are delivering is how to be better prepared, how to answer questions more directly, or how to present information more effectively. Unfortunately, what this type of leader fails to understand is that the lessons they are teaching are far different and very damaging.

Are your leaders "teaching" your employees any of the following dangerous and counterproductive lessons?

Lesson One: Do Not Share Bad News.

If an employee presents information from a project she is working on and is publicly chastised for poor data or results, the chances are excellent that future data of that type will not see the light of day. Her goal in the future will be to either hide data that is contrary to the hypothesis that the leaders are trying to prove, or to remove herself from the position of having to present results.

She has learned that it is dangerous to share bad news.

Lesson Two: Don't Surface a Problem Until You Have a Solution.

While many leaders tell their people, quite rightly, that they should not just come with a problem, they should come with a solution as well, this can be taken to an illogical extreme.

In one company I worked with, a significant problem had surfaced in a major capital project. The lead engineer on the team knew that this problem could potentially derail the entire effort, which was within weeks of a significant capital infusion. The problem surfaced outside of the normal project channels and the lead engineer admitted, upon questioning, that the problem existed but that he had not shared it in the periodic project reviews with upper management.

Due to the reputation of the project leader, I was incredulous and asked him why he had let the project come so close to failure. He told me that he had been trained not to surface a problem without a solution and that he did not have a solution at that time.

Fear of violating a corporate rule kept this very intelligent man from doing what he knew was in the best interest of the company.

Lesson Three: Don't Let the Hot Potato Fall in Your Lap.

This lesson forces people throughout the organization to continue to "do their part" on a project that has flaws and work to get it off of their desks. They ensure that the problem doesn't surface on "their watch."

I have had employees advise me of a problem in a particular product or process but swear me to secrecy because they felt that if it were discovered that they surfaced the contrary information, they would be disciplined or even terminated. These employees would rather just do what they could and let the chips fall where they may, even if it meant that the problem was found much later and cost the company, and perhaps its customers, more money.

An effective leader who finds himself working in a fear-based culture has a difficult and important job. He must find ways to reward employees who take prudent risks and who raise issues.

When projects are off track or failing, the leader worth following finds a way to discuss the problem unemotionally and in private with the project leader. What is the issue? Is the project flawed in some way? Are there too few resources being applied? Does the project have competing objectives?

Probing for these answers in a non-emotional way will lead to better information. Better information will help the effective leader find a way to solve the problem and get the project back on track.

Yes, results are critical and sometimes tough decisions need to be made when a project leader does not deliver. The effective leader will know when to take aggressive action and when to have patience if he treats each situation as a unique opportunity to learn and partner with his team versus berating them for lack of progress. The effective leader will know the difference between a project leader who consistently makes mistakes or doesn't deliver and one who has a great track record of results but who has hit a snag on his current project.

Many leaders in "big jobs" are impatient "Type A" personalities. While the aggressive "Type A" typically is quite productive and gets things done, he often leaves a long line of bodies in his path. If you have leaders on your team with this tendency, coach them to balance their desire to achieve and move on, with the desire to get the best information so that the next step is clearer.

Principle Five: Action Steps

Action Step One:
Evaluate Your Own Behavior

The first key step to eliminating fear in your organization is to objectively evaluate your own behavior. The organizational climate is usually set from the top. If the culture is fear-based and closed, it may be that you are sending an unhealthy message to your leadership team.

Do you have a trusted advisor in your firm? Do you have an open relationship with a board member or your human resources leader? Perhaps you have worked with an industrial psychologist from time to time who understands the culture in your organization. Spend some time talking to your advisor about the culture. How is your behavior perceived? Are you seen as aggressive, busy, and unapproachable? Do you have a reputation for firing or demeaning those who disagree with you?

If, in the course of these conversations, it becomes clear that your behavior may be part of the problem, talk with your leadership team candidly about your desire to make appropriate changes. Advise your team that it is your belief that a more open culture could be beneficial to operations and results. Detail for them what changes you will make. Examples may include:

- You will always give an idea a fair hearing and reasonable debate prior to making a decision on its viability

- You will avoid attacking statements when you are challenging an assumption or conclusion. (i.e., you will say, "I am not clear on how you arrived at that conclusion. Can you provide me with more detail?" rather than saying, "You cannot possibly defend that conclusion based on the data.")

- You will avoid threatening statements such as, "If you can't figure out how to solve this problem, I will find someone who can."

Ask your team what other changes you could make in order to be a more approachable leader.

Action Step Two:
Involve Your Team in the Solution

Work with your leadership team to further eliminate fear in your organization. Some teams have used the "Stop, Start, Continue" exercise with success. In this exercise, each team member shares with the others what he or she would like them to stop, start, or continue doing. This helps each member of the team get a better idea of what behaviors are effective and what behaviors are destructive. This exercise can be specifically tailored to the issue of fear in the workplace.

Challenge the entire leadership team to demonstrate more open and approachable behavior in group meetings. If an employee is struggling with a project, encourage your leaders to ask what is needed in order to be more successful rather than berating lack of results. Remind them that while it is appropriate to let employees know that you are disappointed in the results, it is counterproductive to infer that you are disappointed in them or consider them stupid or lazy.

Do not infer that this more open and approachable behavior somehow translates into less accountability. Accountability is critical in any organization. By maintaining your composure in a group setting, however, you are far more likely to get the true results, true information and appropriate accountability.

As you and your leadership team make changes in how you approach employees and each other, fear will gradually lessen in the organization. It will take time, however, especially if there has been a long history of fear in the culture.

Principle Six: Manage Consensus

What is the "consensus culture" in the organization? Are employees eager to present new ideas and have them debated or do people wait to see which way the wind is blowing and try to adopt the prevailing wisdom?

In effectively executing a business strategy, it is critical that the key leaders be "lined up" with the plan. It is imperative that they have aligned themselves and their teams with what the business needs to accomplish. At the execution stage, there is no longer room for debate, or even reluctant compliance.

An effective leader knows, however, that consensus prior to the execution phase, when the ideas and strategies are still being fleshed out, is very dangerous.

Resist Early Consensus

Early consensus is usually a symptom of fear, lack of confidence, or lack of trust in the leader. Particularly if the leader is quite outspoken in his or her opinions and beliefs, subordinates will agree with the position and not risk voicing disagreement. As a result, good ideas, vital information, and changes in the marketplace are not incorporated into the plans of the organization. This can have serious consequences for the effectiveness of a business strategy.

Over the years, I have participated in a number of staff meetings wherein the leader raised an issue or asked a question and the topic was met with silence. Typically, there are one or two people who will eventually express an opinion to get the conversation going and determine how the leader feels about the topic. Once the leader's position becomes clear, the group lines up behind the leader. It is very difficult for one or two staff members to disagree with that amount of contrary energy.

Even if he feels that staff members supporting the contrary view are incorrect, an effective leader thanks the dissenting members for helping the group to see the other side of the issue and recognizes the courage it took for them to stand behind their convictions.

The effective leader will also take the time to ask for debate. She will tolerate ideas that seem "off the wall" in the brainstorming process. She will understand that there may be many ways to attack a problem and her way is not automatically the best because she has the biggest job in the room.

One business owner shared with me his technique for ensuring that his ideas were thoroughly debated by the team. He presents an idea and then says, "OK, in the next twenty minutes, tell me everything that is wrong with it." His employees have the opportunity to influence his decisions and he is secure in the knowledge that his ideas will not be blindly implemented just because they are his.

At the risk of being redundant, however, I must stress that after the debate is over, ideas have been evaluated and the group has reached a consensus, the leader cannot tolerate a team member backsliding, grumbling to his peers or subordinates, or undermining the group's decisions. The effective leader deals swiftly with this lack of teamwork.

Nurture New Ideas

Companies often debate the wisdom of hiring new and fresh ideas from the outside versus promoting talented people from within. Both strategies have merit, and a mix of each is usually best.

If a work group or leadership team has been together for a long time, however, a company may not reap the benefits of the creative, new people who have been brought into the firm. In many cases, new ideas will be not be objectively considered. In one company with which I worked, we affectionately called this the "The Body Rejecting the Organ" Syndrome.

In time, a new person who has been brought in to add an "outside" perspective will become frustrated and leave the organization if constantly told that, "That won't work here," "That may have worked in your previous industry but not in this one," "We tried that ten years ago and it didn't work," "We are different." Losing an employee who becomes frustrated by the lack of change within the firm not only is a huge waste of money and time, it makes it that much more difficult for the next newcomer to be successful.

One very effective leader I worked with recognized that a "new organ" that he had specifically recruited to add some creativity into an area that had grown a bit stale was in danger of being rejected due to the lack of support he was receiving from a peer who had spent considerable time in the function. In overt and covert ways, the new employee was being undermined. The leader took the long-term employee aside and charged him with the responsibility for making this new employee successful. If the new leader failed, so did the established one. This improved the situation overnight.

Principle Six:
Action Steps

Action Step One:
Solicit Information

Prior to making a good decision, it is imperative that you consider all available, relevant information adequately. Certainly I am not advocating "analysis paralysis," which tends to plague people or organizations who cannot make a decision until every angle, detail and possibility has been evaluated.

Rather, I advocate ensuring that major decisions get an open and adequate hearing. As the leader, you have ample opportunity to solicit feedback from your team on major decisions.

Perhaps you are considering a major acquisition. As you have researched the firm you have identified for purchase, you have focused on the great strategic fit between your organizations. Discuss this potential purchase with your leadership team. Ask for their candid opinions about this acquisition.

- Is this the right time to take on an integration of this size?
- Is the firm well thought of in the marketplace?
- What is the condition of their balance sheet?
- Will there be considerable redundancy in functions and staff? How will redundancy be handled?

Listen to their input and ask for further information where warranted. By making it clear that you need and want all available information, you increase your likelihood of making a good decision. Some leaders may be concerned about sharing this type of information too broadly. If you have leaders on your direct staff who cannot maintain confidentiality about these types of business decisions, you have the wrong team members.

Action Step Two:
Encourage Your Leadership Team to Solicit Information

Once you have modeled this behavior with your leadership team, make sure that they are using the same technique when making decisions in their own functions. When one of your leaders comes to you and says that he or she wants to implement a new process, ask who else had been involved in the discussion. What do the other department heads think about the change? How will the change affect the workload or efficiency of other departments? What do key departmental employees think about the change? Have the views of customers or suppliers been considered?

Again, your objective is not to slow decision-making. Your objective is to manage consensus so that your team makes better decisions, the first time. Companies often find that the time that they were unable to take at the beginning of a project, they are forced to take at the end as they correct mistakes.

Action Step Three:
Examine Failures

A final suggestion in learning how to manage consensus better is to examine why a new project or process failed. What new information surfaced in the midst of the project that was missed at the beginning? By taking the time to understand what you didn't know and how to ensure that you gather that data the next time, you will reduce your chances for a repeat failure.

Principle Seven: Be Candid

Is it possible to "speak the truth" in your organization? Does the culture in your organization encourage open, honest, and compassionate feedback to both correct mistakes and inspire performance?

"Telling it like it is" is becoming a dying art in Corporate America. Certainly confrontation is never easy. It is difficult to tell someone calmly and directly that his or her performance is below par or that behavior is inappropriate. I believe that being candid has become even tougher in a society so attuned to "political correctness." Women and minorities in particular often do not get the coaching that they need to improve their performance because their managers fear being labeled a sexist or a racist.

A manager I worked with for many years had a subordinate who was African-American. The subordinate was very talented and her boss felt that she could take on more responsibility. Her one performance issue was that she was relatively inarticulate and the lack of ability to get her ideas across was eroding her effectiveness. While her boss wanted to help her and at first seemed willing to have the conversation, he finally decided that, as a white male, it was too risky for him to discuss it with her.

I was working recently with a very bright woman who was alienating herself from her peers and superiors with her aggressive and abrasive manner. While her boss had solicited considerable feedback that could have helped her, he chose not to share it with her until several key leaders in the company told him that they would no longer work with her. To his credit, at that point he hired a coach to help her, but the damage was so severe by then that recovery took longer than it might have had the situation been dealt with earlier.

In a third instance, a female employee was coming to work on a relatively frequent basis in clothing that was inappropriate. Her boss felt that, because he was a male, his comments about the inappropriate attire could be misinterpreted. The candid conversation was delegated to a person in human resources. Given the fact that the behavior did not appreciably change, it appeared that the feedback was not accepted as credible. This talented woman was eroding her chances for further advancement and her boss was not candid enough to level with her.

Women and minorities are not the only employees who suffer due to a lack of feedback, however. All employees can benefit by regular conversations with their managers which point out what they are doing well and how they are damaging their credibility or effectiveness.

It has been my experience that the higher a person ascends in an organization, the less likely it is that she will give candid feedback. So often, as a human resources professional, I have been asked to provide feedback to peer staff members who are exhibiting either performance problems or inappropriate behavior on the job because the boss was unwilling to do so.

This is not true in all cases, certainly. A colleague recently shared with me how effectively her boss, the owner of the company, had handled a delicate performance issue. A very good employee had been accused of behaving inappropriately with a group of subordinates. Rather than delegating the task of performance feedback, the owner traveled to the employee's work location, met with the employee personally and confronted the employee with the accusation. The owner expressed his displeasure with the situation, and his confidence that the employee could overcome the issue. He then outlined what resources would be available to the employee. I believe that this employee's chances of becoming a productive member of the team have risen considerably due to the owner's hands-on approach.

Address Performance "Real Time"

Effective leaders recognize that allowing performance issues to fester significantly erodes morale and reduces the effectiveness of the team. More often than not, an employee will welcome the feedback and make efforts to correct the deficient behavior.

It is critical to give this feedback "real time". Many managers wait until the annual performance review to unload a year's worth of issues on an employee who thought things were going fairly well. This "surprise" damages the relationship between the manager and the employee.

One employee told me that her boss had spent the entire previous year making detailed notes of every missed project deadline, every work product that did not meet expectations and every missed day of work that created issues for the rest of the work team.

These observations were given to her in her annual performance review, which lasted three hours. The employee shared her frustration with me, indicating that she was ready to walk off the job after that experience.

When performance reviews are done, good leaders ensure that they are delivering fair and actionable feedback. Rather than just focus on deficiencies, they highlight both what was done well over the past year and what needs improvement. They set the next year's goals with their employee's input and challenge the employee to achieve higher levels of performance. An effective leader also takes the opportunity to talk to the employee about career goals. She explores what the employee would like to do next or would like to learn.

Be a Coach

I have had the pleasure of working for a number of excellent leaders and mentors. Each of them took the time to give me performance feedback.

One of my mentors told me, when I had been complaining about the lack of women in higher level positions in our firm, that I had to decide whether I was going to become part of the problem or part of the solution. That comment helped me realize that if I was going to achieve the higher levels I aspired to, I would have to change my attitude and concentrate on demonstrating my competence. Within a year of that tough conversation, I was awarded my first promotion.

Another mentor helped me to become more "tough-minded," a key skill I needed to develop as I assumed more responsibility in the organization.

A third mentor quietly shared a piece of wisdom with me that I use and repeat often. As I talked with him about an employee investigation I was doing, I marveled that I had witnessed two people who were in the same interaction and who walked away with entirely opposite points of view. "And the truth is somewhere in the middle," he said. That simple insight has served me very well over the years.

I have heard employees complain over the years that the "company should give them a mentor." While some companies have established effective mentoring programs, employees who wish to have a coach or mentor do not have to wait for the company to establish a formal process. My best mentors were talented leaders with whom I had the pleasure of working. Our "mentoring sessions" were typically an informal cup of coffee together when we saw each other in the hallway.

Don't Fall Victim to "Cronyism"

I define "cronyism" as misplaced loyalty. Certainly, if you have worked with someone for a long time who has produced consistently above-average results, you would feel comfortable promoting that person or giving her new challenges. That is well-placed loyalty.

Cronyism rewards a subordinate simply because he has been loyal to you. Perhaps he has failed in one position. You feel that because he has been a good solider for a long time, it is only right that you place him in another job.

Perhaps a former colleague comes to you after failing in another venture. You really don't have a position available but you create a job for her in recognition of your past association.

This behavior is dangerous to the business on many levels. First, your preference for a friend can be viewed as anything from favoritism to discrimination, opening your business to liability.

Second, the "crony" may not be capable of the job to which he or she is assigned, eroding both the overall effectiveness of the company and the morale of the workforce.

Lastly, carrying extra people in today's competitive environment is dangerous to a company's financial health.

A very wise mentor of mine always said that you had, first and foremost, a business relationship with your subordinates. If you were lucky enough to develop a friendship with them, too, that was fine. But both sides of the relationship need to understand that it was the business relationship that came first as long as the boss/subordinate relationship existed. He called that his "separation of church and state." It served him well.

Define the Rules

Each organization has its own "career busters." These are the things that employees say or do that destroy their chances of getting ahead. People who have been in the organization for a long time, may not even recognize them until somebody violates one. Unfortunately, employees can violate one of these unwritten rules, not recognize that they have committed a "career buster," and stay on the job for many years wondering why they cannot get ahead.

An effective leader would do well to examine those "career busters" and help his team understand what they are.

Do you have a subordinate you just hate to see coming because he cannot get to the point and he wastes so much of your time? Tell him that he needs to work at being more concise. As he practices that new skill, give him feedback.

Do you have a subordinate who springs new ideas on your staff at meetings without reviewing these concepts with you first? Discuss the protocol that you prefer with her.

Perhaps you have a subordinate who always is "lobbing a grenade" in your office and expecting you to deal with the fallout. Sit down with this person and let him know that he is responsible for these problems and while you are willing to provide assistance if needed, if he cannot handle most issues without you, he is not providing the leadership necessary in his position.

I worked with a company that had an unwritten rule about meeting start times for the executive group. If the meeting notice said that the meeting was to start at 7:00 a.m. with a continental breakfast and the formal agenda beginning at 7:30 a.m., the meeting would nearly always start at 7:10 or 7:15 a.m. Long-time members of the team would never remember to let the new members know about this aberration and so many of the new people would come into a discussion that had already begun. While we knew that being late was a "career buster" at that firm, together we learned that being simply "on time" wasn't good enough either.

A very effective leader with whom I worked opened his first staff meeting by laying out his expectations of each of us. He talked about one issue: trust. He told each of us that if he couldn't trust us, he didn't need us. He let us know in that conversation that we had a decision to make: we were either on the team, or off of the team. There was no middle position to choose.

Terminate Problem Performers

Terminating employees has become much more difficult as the "employment at will" concept for salaried people erodes. I have worked with companies that carry non-productive employees on their payroll for a long time because they feel it would be too risky from a legal perspective to terminate them.

Human Resources professionals in particular have a reputation for putting stumbling blocks in the way of managers who need more talented or more motivated employees in order to deliver the results that the business needs.

In my experience, the vast number of people whom their managers want to "terminate immediately" haven't suddenly stopped performing. They weren't great employees yesterday and horrible employees today. Typically, the same issues that are causing the problems now have been there for a number of years and the manager has failed to address them. For years, such employees have been getting reasonable performance reviews and modest salary increases.

Suddenly, something changes. Maybe the manager simply does not want to tolerate it anymore or the manager's boss makes a disparaging comment about the person. Often, a new manager has taken over the department. Now, the manager wants to terminate the employee.

An employment scenario like this one is very difficult to win if the former employee brings an action against the company. The legal system will apply the standard of fairness. Did this employee know that she had a performance problem? Was she told that her employment was at risk if she did not make some significant changes quickly? Was she given clear and achievable goals to complete within a reasonable timeframe? Is this process documented?

A company finds itself in a difficult position if managers and leaders do not have on-going conversations with employees to let them know honestly how their performance is viewed.

One of my early lessons on how effective a strong feedback process could be came from a new plant manager at a facility in another state. Shortly after this new plant manager came on board, my office began to get a myriad of legal charges protesting a number of employment terminations. I became concerned about the company's ability to prevail against all of the charges.

This plant manager was able to defend each of the legal challenges by demonstrating with clear and concise paperwork that he had spoken to the employees, given them their goals, met with them periodically, informed them where they were and were not making progress, warned them when it became clear that they were failing, and followed through on the consequences of failure to perform.

Leaders would do well to assess the level of candor in their organization. Do team members have the skills to identify behaviors or performance that is below expectations and coach employees to a higher level?

Principle Seven: Action Steps

Action Step One:
Establish an Effective Performance Management System

Critical to the success of your organization is an effective performance management system. Effective systems can range from very simple to very complex, and they all have the following important components:

- **Performance Planning**

  Before employees can perform to expectations, each must understand what is expected of them. Your employees deserve a discussion at least once a year on what you expect from them and what "meeting or exceeding expectations" looks like in your company.

- **Frequent Feedback**

  This feedback can be formal or informal, but it is important for employees to know how they are doing, especially at critical project milestones. Leaders who say, "Well, if you were not doing a good job, you'd know," are failing in their responsibility to give real-time feedback when things are going well and when performance is below expectations.

- **Annual Performance Feedback**

  At least once a year, you and your leaders should be having formal and written discussions about each employee's performance. This feedback should be directly related to the expectations that you discussed at the beginning of the year. Where did the employee do well and where is there room for improvement? The key rule of thumb in this annual review is that there should be NO SURPRISES! If your employee is genuinely surprised by some feedback that they received in the review, you have not done an adequate job throughout the year of talking with them about their performance.

An employment attorney recently shared, in an employment law update that I attended, that employees often file lawsuits against companies if their employment was terminated and they were unaware that the company was unhappy with their performance. This attorney went on to acknowledge that many managers lack the coaching skills required to adequately address performance problems. He also observed that companies must ensure that they have an open and candid corporate culture that makes these tough conversations part of a good performance management system.

The annual review should be followed up by performance planning for the following year.

If you wish to implement an even more effective performance management system, I would recommend the following enhancements to the basic components listed above:

- **360 Feedback**

  By soliciting feedback from an employee's superiors, peers and subordinates, the performance review will reflect a wider view of the employee's day-to-day performance. Perhaps an employee is very good at "managing up," but consistently alienates those who work for him. The 360-feedback process would reveal that development need.

- **Values Feedback**

  Performance management systems that measure not only what is accomplished, but how it is accomplished, help you, as the leader, set the tone for your workplace. If teamwork and integrity are key values for you, measure your subordinates on those behaviors.

- **Two-Level Review**

  If you are unsure how accurately or how candidly your leaders are completing performance reviews, you may wish to institute a two-level review process. This ensures that, prior to an employee receiving a performance evaluation, the evaluation is reviewed by another layer of management. This provides for more consistent ratings throughout the organization.

Action Step Two: Improve Coaching Skills

Perhaps, in addition to improving your performance management process, you wish to improve the coaching skills of your leadership team. Consider hosting a series of informal roundtables to discuss coaching opportunities or performance issues that your leaders may be facing within their teams. By soliciting peer feedback, leaders are often better equipped to coach a problem employee. You may want to consider bringing in an outside facilitator to lead your roundtable discussions.

Action Step Three:
Identify Career Busters

Lastly, spend some time with your leadership team defining the career busters in your organization. It may be the first time that you have actually thought about and articulated what derails a career in your organization. By defining those career busters for your entire team, your leaders can better manage their own behavior and the behavior of their subordinates.

Principle Eight: Communicate

O ne of the biggest trust killers in Corporate America is the "need to know" mantra. Certainly, not every piece of information about the company, its strategy and its plans can be public knowledge. As a former CEO of mine said, "Business is War." A company's market advantage can be easily eroded if its competitors have access to vital information.

It is my belief, however, that there is a good deal of information that could be shared that is not. Each company has its own culture and all share information in different ways. In a company I was working with recently, employees of the firm often called me to see if I would tell them what was going on because the leaders of the firm were not sharing information.

It is human nature to assume the worst when there is a lack of information. Countless hours had been wasted in this organization by employees talking both on and off company time about their dire predictions. Turnover accelerated over a six-month period due to the uncertainty of the company's future.

Share General Information

While opinions vary widely on how much information a company should share, I believe the most effective leaders share as much information as possible without putting the company at risk.

High-level strategic plan summaries, financial data, new customer prospects and changes to the competitive landscape are all pieces of information that are important for employees to know and to understand. Only employees informed about the challenges of the business can make appropriate decisions on a daily basis.

In one firm I worked with, the executive team would discuss, prior to the start of the fiscal year, a list of items that were critical to achieving the fiscal year budget. These items then became the focal point for communication to employees throughout the year. These communication updates were frequent reminders to all employees on what was important and it gave them updates on how the company was doing against those critical items.

Hold consistent periodic meetings that employees can count on. Companies often restart communications initiatives following a poor employee survey, during a union drive or before union negotiations. Employees see these efforts for what they are: short-term fixes to get the firm through a difficult situation.

A long-term commitment to a communication plan lets employees know that they are valuable members of the team.

Enable Two-Way Communication

Many leaders, when challenged on their communication style say, "Well, we have a monthly meeting and I tell them what is going on. What more do they want?" The effective leader knows that true communication is two-way. This leader solicits information informally by walking around the facility and engaging employees in conversation. The leader gains an accurate sense of the workload, the morale, the challenges and the frustrations by mingling with the people that do the work each day.

A note of caution to this engaging leader: it is critically important to properly manage the information that is gleaned on these tours. If you use information that you gained to criticize an employee's boss or question the department's direction, it is certain that the employee that shared the information will not only be chastised, he or she will not talk with you again. It is the mark of a good leader to be able to act on critical information gained without closing off its sources.

I have often thought how sad it is that companies have resorted to periodic, electronic, anonymous employee surveys to assess the morale of the work group. Certainly, especially in large firms with employees in a number of places, it is hard to have a good pulse on the entire work group.

If, however, the company is practicing good two-way communication, its leaders are out in the facilities talking to their people, it has an open-door policy and it has leaders who are approachable and respectful, the survey data will only confirm what a company already knows.

I had the pleasure of working with a leader who had an interesting technique of drawing out the ideas of the person with whom he was in conversation. He would ask a question and the other person would answer. This leader would then pause and maintain eye contact a bit longer than was comfortable. The pause would prompt the other person to start talking again. I am sure this effective leader gleaned much more detailed, usable information because he had the patience to stay with the conversation just past when it was comfortable.

An effective leader is engaging her employees in the business on a consistent basis. When the company lands that new account, secures a price increase or launches a new service, by communicating those successes, she is helping them feel that this is an integral part of what they do every day. She is developing loyalty both to the organization and to herself.

Principle Eight:
Action Steps

Action Step One:
Develop a Communication Plan

Developing a well-thought-out communication plan is a good first step in sharing more information with your organization. You and your leadership team need to make several key decisions regarding your plan:

- **What should we share?**

  Your employees are interested in all aspects of your business. Information about strategy, customers, competitors, suppliers, new market developments, technology advances, market share, new services, acquisitions, new employee programs, profitability and problems facing the business are all excellent topics to cover. While the likelihood of this information getting into the hands of competitors is remote, be sure that there is a mechanism in place to ensure that confidential company information is not being put at risk.

- **How often should we host a meeting?**

  Companies approach this differently. Some host an annual meeting to bring employees up to speed on year-end results. Other companies host quarterly meetings. I believe a one-hour information meeting once a month with some additional time for questions and answers with a senior executive gives employees the real-time information that they need to make good decisions on behalf of the business.

- **How do we reach beyond the headquarters?**

  If you have employees in other locations, don't forget that they need the same information! In fact, they might need it more due to the fact that they are one step removed from the headquarters. You could have each of your facility leaders do a similar presentation on site or you could use various types of technology to enable these communications.

  Explore with your technical people what other sorts of communications are enabled by your computer or telecommunications architecture.

Action Step Two:
Ensure Two-Way Communication

There is a variety of ways to ensure that communication is two-way in your organization. If you lead a large, far-flung organization, you may want to consider an anonymous employee survey. This type of survey can also be helpful if you are new in your leadership position and you want to get a "snapshot" of morale in your organization. If you feel that you have some leaders that are not performing up to expectations, a well-designed and administered survey can identify those types of problem areas, as well.

The most effective two-way communication process is having an "open door." By being visible in the workplace and letting people know that you are accessible and interested, you will generate the type of information that is critical to running your business effectively.

Creating opportunities for employees to meet with you informally is an effective way of reinforcing your "open door" policy. Many companies host a casual monthly gathering at which a rotating group of employees meet informally over breakfast or coffee with the organization's leaders for conversation and Q&A.

Part Three
Developing and Maintaining the Team

The Principles

E ffective leaders recognize that their current and future "shining stars" desire professional growth: more responsibility, more challenging and visible projects, more exposure to various part of the business and more money. This growth typically leads to more hours, more travel, more work stress, more home issues and the long-term potential for burnout.

Understanding how to both grow people and model behaviors for optimum long-term performance is the responsibility of the team leader.

In this section I will highlight two development principles:

Grow Future Leaders

Maintain the Machine

Principle Nine: Grow Future Leaders

Perhaps nothing is as important to the effectiveness of a leader as the quality the people who work on their team. An effective leader understands that she is responsible for the growth and development of the people she supervises.

Generally speaking, employees entering the workplace today are not loyal to an organization. They are loyal to themselves. The common belief is that only by changing jobs will they get the kind of well-rounded experience, upward mobility and compensation that they desire.

While the type of "lifetime employment" that employees and employers formerly enjoyed is becoming increasingly rare, I believe that, if a company invests time, energy and money in strong employee communication and employee development processes, retention rates will improve.

Employees want to grow, they want to understand the big picture, they want to know that what they do every day helps the company survive and thrive. They want to know that there are opportunities to learn new things and take on greater responsibilities.

Hire the Best

Certainly, you want to give your superior employees a chance to get promoted and move up in your organization. It is important, however, to ensure that when you have an open position that you wish to fill, you treat it as the incredible opportunity that it is.

Review the strengths and weaknesses of your team. Dr. Jerry Bell, a professor at Chapel Hill, who is also an author and workshop facilitator, has developed a model that outlines six core skills that talented people possess. In his book, *The Achievers*, Dr. Bell advocates a balance of skills to augment the skill set of the leader and to round out the whole team. If, as an example, you have a core group of very creative people but the output of the department is low, perhaps you would like to hire a person with a "Producer" skill set. According to Dr. Bell, Producers are highly results oriented. A Producer introduced into this team might be able to take some of these good ideas and help bring them to the marketplace.

Many managers tend to hire people that fit a specific need. If they lost an industrial engineer with three years experience, that is what they seek in the marketplace. View the chance to hire someone as a reason to revisit how the department operates; analyze the products and services it delivers, determine new customer demands that may surface, given the company strategy. How can you best utilize that open position?

Look for core skills. A colleague recently shared with me that he was not necessarily looking for the specific functional skill set. He said, "Give me someone who is smart, dedicated and has a strong sense of customer service and I can teach them everything else." In his experience, a positive, pleasant and helpful customer attitude was a core building block for success.

Give your Employees the Spotlight

Some people in leadership positions have held on to the old adage that knowledge is power. They closely guard the most important and most visible tasks for themselves, fearing that if a subordinate gains more expertise, he could easily replace the manager.

These managers also take any opportunity to present department reports or project status to higher-level managers, if the news is positive.

Effective leaders that I have had the pleasure of working with know that a major part of their responsibility is to grow future leaders. That means giving subordinates the visible, challenging roles. It means inviting them to key meetings and allowing them to represent the department or speak. It means giving them big responsibilities to challenge their abilities. It is being willing to help them when help is needed. It means putting your own ego on the side and allowing someone else to grow.

Typically, the best growth opportunities for employees are on-the-job assignments that involve participants from other functions. This enables the whole group to view the organization more broadly and understand more clearly how the work that they do individually benefits the organization as a whole.

Give a group of talented employees a real business problem to discuss, research and solve. Ask them to present their findings and recommendations to top leaders. You will not only increase your leadership reach, you will continue to grow your people.

I was given multiple opportunities to work on these types of projects in my career. I was able to learn about the company and, thereby, increase my knowledge and value. I am certain that one such assignment, which gave me the opportunity to present the group's findings to the leadership team, resulted in my being offered a key promotion in my career.

I have been fortunate to work with companies that have formalized these types of on-the-job development processes. Effective leaders appreciate the chance to nominate their employees for these types of assignments. Employees see it as a great opportunity to learn and to gain exposure to higher-level management.

I recently worked with a company that decided to provide a coach for one of its employees. This employee was technically capable and very dedicated, but lacked some important skills that he would need as he aspired to higher-level positions. The company was investing in its future and the employee recognized that he was being groomed for more responsibility.

Learn to Delegate Well

The ability to delegate well is an art form. Delegation styles range from severe micro-management to total lack of accountability.

I believe that the most difficult part of delegating effectively is remaining accountable. You maintain responsibility if a problem arises.

I learned this lesson the hard way when two of my employees failed to execute a project well and my management was incensed. Although every fiber in my being wanted to blame my subordinates, I recognized that our department failed that task because I was not close enough to the process. I didn't delegate, I dumped.

Those leaders who have learned to delegate well understand that clear objectives, periodic follow-ups and an open-door policy that allows a subordinate who is experiencing problems to come forward, are all critically important.

Institute a Succession Process

While it may be less important in a small family-owned business, most businesses need a succession process.

Several of the best leaders I've encountered clearly stated their expectation that each staff member be responsible for identifying, developing, and grooming successors. These leaders also ensured that periodic reviews were held to assess the success of those efforts.

A succession process, led by the leader, demonstrates to the entire organization that the leader is dedicated to the firm's market success, its long-term viability and the growth and development of its people.

There is considerable debate about whether or not to share with the entire work team who is on the succession plan. I advocate that this process be as transparent as possible. Managers who have employees who are identified to be groomed as successors should immediately sit down with their employees and discuss the process with them. At times, employees may surprise the manager and tell her that they are not interested in higher-level positions or that they actually have a career aspiration in another field. The company can gain valuable insight in talking to their brightest and best as part of the succession process.

I have seen high-potential employees leave a company because they cannot see a future with the firm. Leaders sadly looked at the succession plan and talked about how hard it was to keep good people. Did these employees know that they were deemed to be successors? Were opportunities for additional responsibilities and exposure being offered to them?

I have heard the other side of the argument, as well. If we identify the people who are the successors, how do we deal with those that are not on the list, who have aspirations that are unreasonable? This is a poor reason to keep a succession planning process under wraps. Managers who have employees who are not viewed as high potential people must develop the skills to discuss the situation with the employee and point out where their performance, their attitudes or their skills are not consistent with the high-potential definition.

An effective leader realizes that she is responsible for building a strong team that advances the organization's goals.

Principle Nine: Action Steps

Action Step One:
Analyze your Workforce

Analyzing your current workforce is an important first step in deciding how best to strengthen your current and future team.

While you and your leaders may add other dimensions, key elements to analyze may include:

The Selection Process

Are you hiring the best people available? Review with your team the last 12 professional hires that have been on the job for six months or more. How are they doing? Are they meeting expectations? Do they possess the skills that you recruited? Have any of them resigned or been fired?

Based on this informal analysis, you may want to examine your selection process:

- How do we source candidates?
- Do we get an adequate number of qualified people applying for our positions?
- Do we see adequate diversity in the candidates that apply?
- Are our interviewing techniques effective?

- How is the final decision made?
- Do we use drug and alcohol screens?
- Do we use validated testing?
- Are we using psychological assessments appropriately?

Making changes to your selection process can pay big dividends in the quality of the people you recruit.

Total Rewards

Is your reward package adequate to entice and keep the employees that you want? You may want to review how the total compensation package that you offer to both exempt and non-exempt employees stacks up against other employers in your area. If you lag the market, you may find yourself in a situation of training employees for other employers.

Remember that it is not just the hourly wage or the salary of the position that make up the rewards package. How does your firm compare to others in your area in terms of medical plan coverage and cost, dental or vision coverage, paid time off or retiree benefits?

I learned the hard way that younger workers care far more about the base wage than they do about any of the other benefits that you may offer. If your firm is established and you have great family medical benefits, a great retirement plan and you pay average to the market, don't be surprised of you have difficulty recruiting younger employees. They may go down the street to the employer who has a higher base wage but just a bare bones medical and retirement package.

Think through these issues with your team, especially if you are opening a new facility.

Average tenure in key technical areas

Are you in a situation wherein a large majority of your technical talent and institutional knowledge is going to retire within the next two or three years? What are you and your team doing now to recruit new talent, capture institutional knowledge and provide for a smooth transition?

By identifying future gaps now, you can hire people and match them up with incumbents who can train them, arrange for employment contracts with future retirees, use data warehousing to store key technical knowledge and/or determine whether purchasing this expertise from another firm is viable or advisable.

Skill gaps

If your organization has a history of promoting people from within, you may find that your team lacks skills in a specific area. As an example, perhaps your company has historically gone to market by private labeling for a retailer or wholesaler. If, as part of your long-term strategy, you decide to go directly to market with your own name, your firm may lack marketing and sales expertise. These may be gaps that you will have to fill in the outside job market.

Examine your strategic plan. What changes are you making or forecasting that will impact the types of skills that you will need?

Key successor gaps

If your company is like many others, very few of your key leadership positions have successors identified who are "ready now." Perhaps there aren't any logical successors in-house for several key positions.

Action Step Two:
Launch Leadership Development Processes

You and your leaders can begin to prepare now by identifying people within the organization who are capable of and interested in assuming leadership roles in the future. Once these "high-potential" employees are identified, you and your team can come up with a variety of ways to accelerate their career growth.

One good way to challenge these high-potential employees is to invite them to participate on a multi-functional team. Give them a real business problem/opportunity to explore, such as a possible acquisition or a significant freight cost reduction.

Give the team a reasonable period of time to do their investigation and then ask them to present their recommendations to you and your leadership team. These kinds of assignments allow you to see how these employees think, work as a team, work under deadlines, support their recommendations and present their results.

Your high-potential employees can also benefit from frequent roundtable discussions on a variety of topics. You and your team can choose topics that are most appropriate for your business, and possible choices may include:

- coaching employees;
- how an emerging technology may impact your business;
- improving delegation skills;
- how outsourcing is affecting your industry; and
- how a competitor's strategy is affecting your market approach.

The benefit of these roundtables is expanded if you and your leadership team lead these discussions. Your approachability as a team is heightened as is your exposure to your future leaders.

Your leadership development processes could include many other elements, as well, including:

- Mentoring
- Educational classes
- Job rotations
- Community involvement
- Speaking opportunities

By incorporating a wide variety of developmental opportunities into a leadership development process, your firm can accelerate the growth of your key leaders.

Principle Ten: Maintain the Machine

I t is tough on the body to live and work in Corporate America today. Most executives who work for global companies spend considerable time traveling, much of it overseas. Effective leaders know that in order to operate at peak performance, they need to maintain excellent health.

Sleep

There is a growing sleep deficit among Americans in general and executives are no exception. Rather than reduce our workload, technology now allows the job to be done 24/7 from nearly anywhere in the world.

The common practice among executives who travel internationally is to try and grab some sleep on the plane and time your arrival so that you have an entire workday ahead of you when you land. The theory is that if you go to bed that night in the new country and wake up in "their morning", you are now on their time and you do not experience jet lag. Perhaps it works for others, it never worked for me.

Vacations are no longer restful times to recharge. Traveling with laptops and cell phones is common, for fear of being out of touch for too long.

In one company that I worked with, we laughed that the executives who were on an assignment in another country didn't observe either U.S. holidays or their home country holidays! They had the opportunity to work them all.

Prolonged lack of sleep erodes effectiveness.

Food

While eating the right foods can be difficult at any time, eating correctly when you are traveling presents a particular challenge.

When you are eating out in restaurants constantly, it is difficult to make healthy choices. It is hard to eat only what you want and not everything that is served you. If you are traveling in countries where the dinner hour is much later than you are accustomed to, you may find yourself eating a heavy meal late at night. Often, there are cultural expectations about what you will eat, when you will eat and eating together.

Do not sacrifice your health for the sake of "going along with the work group." Certainly, it is important to be sociable and entertain clients and mingle with your colleagues. Being sociable does not mean that you have to try and eat the 24-ounce porterhouse because everyone else at your table has ordered it.

If possible, find another colleague that shares your desire for healthy eating.

Alcohol

Another good way to erode the effectiveness of the machine is to ply it with alcohol. It can be difficult in today's business environment to escape the cocktail hour, the wine with dinner, the cordials after dinner and the nightcaps.

Certainly, if you have a demonstrated problem with alcohol, you must totally abstain. This can be very difficult and the peer pressure can be enormous.

Even the social drinkers can find themselves a victim of inappropriate peer pressure. If possible, find opportunities to break away from the "group-drink" mentality and engage in a more productive activity.

You will be much more likely to be an effective leader the next day!

Exercise

The benefits of exercise are numerous and bear repeating for a leader who desires to improve performance on and off the job. Regular exercise is critical for maintaining healthy weight, burning off stress and improving heart fitness and longevity.

I have been heartened to see emerging leaders who organize athletic events for their teams when they are together for a meeting. This leader is demonstrating that a healthy lifestyle is a key ingredient to a successful and lengthy career.

Downtime

The late Joseph Campbell, world-renowned author on mythology, appeared in a video series, called *The Power of Myth*, in which he advocated that human beings "follow their bliss." There are those for whom their vocations are their bliss. For others, whose "bliss" lies outside how they support themselves and their families, adequate time to engage in activities that relax them and give them enjoyment can allow these leaders to return to their work re-energized and engaged.

Principle Ten: Action Steps

Action Step One:
Model Health Behaviors

The most significant change that you, as the leader, can make in this area is to model healthy behaviors. A very effective leader I worked for made a habit of coming in early, but he was always gone by 5:00 p.m. His team knew that he worked out without fail after work. The team also knew that he would take only emergency calls after hours or on the weekends. It was clear that he honored his family time and he expected others to do the same. This leader also made it clear when he was leaving work in the middle of the day to go to one of his children's schools for a concert or a conference.

Another great leader always organized athletic events when his leaders were in town from other locations. This gave the team a chance to unwind together, get some exercise, and have some fun rather than just go to happy hour together. This leader was also sensitive to the fact that he had two leaders who were not able to play sports so he arranged alternative activities, as well.

I have witnessed a leadership team that worked out together every lunch hour. It was amazing how many tough issues were addressed on the treadmill.

Upon my promotion into this leadership team, I became aware that they prided themselves on being active and fit. I found myself following their example and I bought exercise equipment for my home and also frequented the company gym. Thanks to the example of my teammates, I reached an improved level of fitness.

Of course, each leader in your organization must take responsibility for his or her own health. You can help them make good choices and stay healthier by offering options at company functions. Make sure that chicken, fish or vegetarian choices are available as entrée options. If alcohol is served, make sure there are other choices, as well. Many companies have worked to reduce their corporate liability by offering alcohol only for a limited time during company functions.

Footnote to the CEO

One of my favorite bosses and probably the best leader I have known was famous for saying, "This isn't social welfare, you know."

Running a business isn't social welfare. It is all about returning value to the shareholders, as a colleague recently reminded me.

I've worked for leaders who believe that embracing the preceding ten principles and making money were mutually exclusive. In my experience, however, the CEO who ignores these ten principles puts their shareholders at risk.

The CEO in any organization is the "keeper of the values," whether those values are written or unwritten.

What are the values that you model for your employees? Are they the same values that are written in the Company annual report or handbook? Do your employees roll their eyes when you say that they are the Company's most important asset?

How does your team measure up against the ten principles? Some of your leaders may have performance gaps that need to be shored up. As I've indicated, many of these principles are "teachable" skills. You can help your leaders delegate better, communicate more effectively and be candid coaches. Together, you can make changes to your corporate culture.

On the other hand, if you have leaders who lack integrity, who do not genuinely care about people, who are arrogant or put themselves before the team, you need to make changes to your leadership group. These principles are not skills that can be easily learned. They reflect the core values of a person and if they are lacking, no amount of training, coaching or cajoling is going to change them.

This is a tough decision. Perhaps one of these leaders is your highest producer. When you need a job done, you give it to this leader because you know that no matter what, the job will get done. It is imperative that you evaluate the short-term payoff of getting this job done against the long term impact to your organization. If you get a critical job done at the expense of the trust of a team of employees or at the expense of a quality product, you are creating a debt that will someday need to get paid.

The Board Meeting

You are not looking forward to this meeting. Results are not good and this will be the third quarter in a row that you have not met your objectives. You did read the leadership book your mentor suggested, however, and you have spent the last four days out of your office, in your facilities, asking questions and listening.

You talked to three engineers who served on the project team that brought the failed equipment from Europe. You asked about the permitting issue and what happened. You were shocked when one of the engineers produced an email that she had sent to the project leader six months before the equipment was delivered raising the exact issue. Not only did the project leader discount her input, but after the project failed, he made sure that she took the blame. You looked over her performance review, which detailed her failure to secure the proper permits and the resulting project failure.

The engineer assured you she would have quit on the spot but she was five months away from full vesting in her pension and 401(k). She has accepted a position at another firm in town; her last day with your company is next Friday.

Nobody in the Information Technology group was either able or willing to shed any light on the programming error that caused the overbilling situation in the second quarter. The VP stated vehemently that it was a software problem and that the vendor was to blame. When you stated that it was your understanding that most of the programming was done in-house, the VP switched gears and blamed the sales department for inadequately documenting what they wanted the system to do.

You finally met the new Director of Quality Assurance. It turns out that she is the sister-in-law of the VP of Sales and Marketing. She has a strong quality background, but has previously been responsible only for identifying and analyzing failures, not strategic quality planning.

You learned a few other interesting things in your four-day tour. The facility with the rumored union organizing attempt lacks an adequate production planning function and in the last six months workers have been sent home ten times due to lack of work. These short weeks are then capped by mandatory weekend overtime to make up the production shortfall.

The business updates that you carefully prepare and deliver to your team each month are not being communicated to the entire team. Employees throughout the organization are not being kept up to date on the business.

The presentation that you have prepared for the Board is quite a bit different than the one you usually give. While you have included all of the key budgetary metrics, you have included a new section on leadership. In it, you highlight three key areas that you have committed to improve before the next meeting.

First, you will examine your hiring and promotion processes. Based on your research, you have leaders in positions for which they are not qualified. By the next meeting, you will make recommendations on how to change the internal processes and you will report on any leadership changes that were made.

Second, you will ensure that monthly communication meetings are being held throughout the firm. In addition, you will develop and implement an effective, two-way communication process that will encourage employees to share their ideas on how to make the operation more effective.

Third, you will launch a leadership development process that will identify and groom people in your organization to be leaders that others trust and want to follow.

As you conclude your remarks to the Board, you advise them that today you do not have all of the answers. You assure them, however, that you have finally begun to ask the right questions.

Bibliography

Internet Resources

New Employer/Employee Equation Survey summary
www.roughnotes.com
April 2005 edition
Article: "Satisfaction (not) guaranteed"

Barry Nixon, President, National Institution for the Prevention of Workplace Violence "Creating a Respectful Environment May Be Your Best Defense"
www.workplaceviolence911.com